RHINO RESCUE!

And More True Stories of Saving Animals

Clare Hodgson Meeker

NATIONAL
GEOGRAPHIC

WASHINGTON, D.C.

The National Geographic Society is one of the world's largest nonprofit scientific and educational organizations. Founded in 1888 to "increase and diffuse geographic knowledge," the Society's mission is to inspire people to care about the planet. It reaches more than 400 million people worldwide each month through its official journal, *National Geographic,* and other magazines; National Geographic Channel; television documentaries; music; radio; films; books; DVDs; maps; exhibitions; live events; school publishing programs; interactive media; and merchandise. National Geographic has funded more than 10,000 scientific research, conservation, and exploration projects and supports an education program promoting geographic literacy.

Staff for This Book
Shelby Alinsky, *Project Editor*
Callie Broaddus, *Art Director*
Ruth Ann Thompson, *Designer*
Bri Bertoia, *Photo Editor*
Brenna Maloney, *Editor*
Paige Towler, *Editorial Assistant*
Rachel Kenny and Sanjida Rashid, *Design Production Assistants*
Tammi Colleary-Loach, *Rights Clearance Manager*
Michael Cassady and Mari Robinson, *Rights Clearance Specialists*
Grace Hill, *Managing Editor*
Alix Inchausti, *Production Editor*
Lewis R. Bassford, *Production Manager*
George Bounelis, *Manager, Production Services*
Susan Borke, *Legal and Business Affairs*

Published by the National Geographic Society
Gary E. Knell, *President and CEO*
John M. Fahey, *Chairman of the Board*
Melina Gerosa Bellows, *Chief Education Officer*
Declan Moore, *Chief Media Officer*
Hector Sierra, *Senior Vice President and General Manager, Book Division*

Senior Management Team, Kids Publishing and Media Nancy Laties Feresten, *Senior Vice President;* Erica Green, *Vice President, Editorial Director, Kids Books;* Amanda Larsen, *Design Director, Kids Books;* Julie Vosburgh Agnone, *Vice President, Operations;* Jennifer Emmett, *Vice President, Content;* Michelle Sullivan, *Vice President, Video and Digital Initiatives;* Eva Absher-Schantz, *Vice President, Visual Identity;* Rachel Buchholz, *Editor and Vice President, NG Kids magazine;* Jay Sumner, *Photo Director;* Amanda Larsen, *Design Director, Kids Books;* Hannah August, *Marketing Director;* R. Gary Colbert, *Production Director*

Digital Laura Goertzel, *Manager;* Sara Zeglin, *Senior Producer;* Bianca Bowman, *Assistant Producer;* Natalie Jones, *Senior Product Manager*

For more information, please visit nationalgeographic.com, call 1-800-NGS LINE (647-5463), or write to the following address:

National Geographic Society
1145 17th Street N.W.
Washington, D.C. 20036-4688 U.S.A.

Visit us online at nationalgeographic.com/books

For librarians and teachers: ngchildrensbooks.org

National Geographic supports K–12 educators with ELA Common Core Resources. Visit natgeoed.org/commoncore for more information.

More for kids from National Geographic: kids.nationalgeographic.com

For information about special discounts for bulk purchases, please contact National Geographic Books Special Sales: ngspecsales@ngs.org

For rights or permissions inquiries, please contact National Geographic Books Subsidiary Rights: ngbookrights@ngs.org

Trade paperback
ISBN: 978-1-4263-2311-9
Reinforced library edition
ISBN: 978-1-4263-2312-6

Printed in China
15/RRDS/1

Table of CONTENTS

Honey Girl, a Hawaiian monk seal, looks back before diving into the ocean.

HONEY GIRL: MIRACULOUS MONK SEAL!

Having "hauled out" on a sandy beach in Hawaii, this female monk seal warms herself in the sun.

November 2012
Oahu, Hawaii

A kite surfer squinted into the sun. The waves were pretty good that day off the northeastern coast of Oahu (sounds like oh-WAH-hoo) in Hawaii. Suddenly, something caught his eye. There, bobbing in the waves just ahead of him, was a strange sight.

It looked like a monk seal. But this monk seal was green. And it wasn't moving. It looked like the seal was tangled up in something. The surfer wasn't sure what was going on, but one thing was clear: This seal was in trouble.

When the surfer reached land, the first thing he did was call the Hawaiian monk seal hotline. The hotline is part of the National Oceanic and Atmospheric Administration (NOAA) Fisheries Service. He described what he'd seen to wildlife biologist Tracy Mercer. Tracy is in charge of NOAA's monk seal search and rescue operations on the main Hawaiian Islands. Since 2002, she's been working with a team of NOAA scientists, staff, and volunteers to keep track of this endangered population of Hawaiian monk seals. The team also rescues injured seals so they can be treated and returned to the wild. Tracy sent a search team to the spot where the surfer had seen the seal. They found nothing.

Five days later, a NOAA response team volunteer sent photos of a monk seal lying on a beach not far from where the injured seal had first been spotted. The seal was dangerously thin, and it looked green.

Tracy studied the photo. Her heart sank as she read the tag on the monk seal's flipper: R5AY. She knew this seal. It was Honey Girl, a 17-year-old female. Honey Girl was well known to the NOAA staff and volunteers.

At Home in Rough Waters

Monk seals are native to Hawaii. They aren't found anywhere else in the world. The northeastern coast of Oahu is known for its big waves and rough water. When storms roll in from the Pacific Ocean, most animals take cover. But the monk seal is built for this rugged environment. It has a sleek, barrel-shaped body and powerful back flippers. It can glide through strong ocean currents and dive deep for food. Ancient Hawaiian legends called the monk seal *Ilio holo i ka uaua* (sounds like EE-lee-oh HO-lo i COW ah-OO-ah). It means "the dog that runs in rough seas."

Honey Girl had given birth to seven pups over seven years. Everyone called her a "miracle mom." She had raised each pup with great care. Now Honey Girl was the one in need of care. Tracy knew she had to save her. She also knew she'd need help to do it.

NOAA's on-duty marine mammal veterinarian (sounds like vet-er-ih-NAIR-ee-en) answered the call. Dr. Michelle Barbieri (sounds like bar-bee-AIR-ee) knew a lot about monk seals. At first light, she and Tracy began the long drive to the coast. Hours later, they reached the beach and started their search.

Over the next three days, Tracy, Michelle, and a team of volunteers hiked along a 15-mile (24-km) stretch of coastline, searching. Monk seals spend most of their time in the water, but a healthy seal will spend time on land, too. It's called "hauling out." The team combed the beaches, hoping to find Honey Girl.

Finally, they saw her. She was drifting in the waves offshore. But she was never close enough to the shore for them to reach her. Tracy and Michelle grew anxious (sounds like ANGK-shuhs). "It's suspicious when a monk seal does not haul out and is floating or logging on the water's surface," said Michelle. "Maybe something is preventing her from coming on shore." But what could it be?

They got their answer when they found Honey Girl on the beach a few days later, asleep. "We didn't want to scare her back into the water," said Michelle. As they approached her quietly, they saw the source of Honey Girl's problem.

A fishhook the size of Michelle's palm was lodged into Honey Girl's cheek. A tangle of razor-sharp fishing line trailed from her mouth. Every time she moved, the line cut deeper into her skin.

Finding Honey Girl solved another mystery, too. Tracy and Michelle discovered why Honey Girl looked green. Her coat was covered with mossy, green algae (sounds like AL-jee).

"Algae grows on most seal hair, but it usually bleaches out from their lying in the sun," said Michelle. "Honey Girl must have been floating in the water for several weeks." The sun hadn't bleached it.

Michelle noticed something else, too. Honey Girl's ribs and spine were showing. This meant she had not eaten for a very long time.

This worried Michelle. She knew that Honey Girl had recently weaned a pup. She had already lost half of her body weight from nursing her pup. She needed to eat to regain that weight.

It was clear that Honey Girl needed immediate help. There was no way to tell at that moment how much damage the fishing line had done. At least Michelle could trim away some of the line to make things less painful for Honey Girl.

Michelle and Tracy decided to transport Honey Girl to the Waikiki (sounds like WHY-kee-kee) Aquarium.

It was the only place on Oahu that treated injured marine mammals.

Honey Girl was hurt, but she was also probably pretty scared, too. The rescue team needed to move carefully but quickly.

Moving an injured monk seal is a tough challenge. Even at half her normal weight, Honey Girl weighed more than 300 pounds (136 kg). The team used a large plank of wood with a handle on the back to gently guide her into a metal cage.

Once Honey Girl was inside the cage, it took six people to lift it onto the back of a truck. Honey Girl opened her eyes but showed little reaction to the people around her. As the truck drove off, everyone was wondering if Honey Girl would make it. Would she ever see the ocean again?

Rescuers watch as Honey Girl wriggles out of a carrying cage and makes her way back to the ocean.

Chapter 2

A Delicate OPERATION

At the Waikiki Aquarium, Honey Girl was given medicine to make her feel drowsy. Only now was it safe for Michelle to gently open her mouth and look inside. The fishing line had left her tongue swollen and deeply infected. It was hard to know how far the infection had spread. Honey Girl would need surgery to repair the damage.

Performing surgery on any wild animal can be dangerous. It's especially hard on a monk seal. The same dive reflex that allows a seal to stay underwater for a long time could cause her to stop breathing when she's put to sleep for surgery. Michelle needed an experienced doctor. She called on Dr. Miles Yoshioka at the Honolulu Zoo. He agreed to take the job.

Miles took a look at Honey Girl. The infection had not spread beyond her tongue. That was the good news. But much of her tongue was damaged beyond repair. Miles had to cut away nearly two-thirds of Honey Girl's tongue. The next few days after the surgery would be critical. No one knew if Honey Girl would survive.

Honey Girl was moved to an empty pool to recover. For two days after the surgery, she barely moved at all. Michelle didn't know if Honey Girl was ready to swim yet, so they kept the tank empty of water.

Honey Girl was weak and dehydrated. Michelle injected fluids under her skin to rehydrate her. She gave her more pain medication to soothe her swollen tongue. None of these treatments seemed to help.

On the third day, Michelle filled the empty pool with water. As soon as the water was high enough for her to float, Honey Girl started swimming. Michelle and the aquarium staff were thrilled to see her moving again. But Michelle was also cautious (sounds like CAW-shus). She knew Honey Girl was weak. She made sure that a staff member was always nearby, in case Honey Girl struggled in the water or started to sink.

But instead of showing signs of weakness, Honey Girl seemed to grow stronger in the water. She also tried to bite her caretakers with her sharp teeth. This was a very good sign. It meant that Honey Girl was responding the way a wild animal should when near humans.

Now they needed Honey Girl to start eating again to gain back her strength. Michelle used a tube to feed Honey Girl a meal of pureed (sounds like pure-AID) herring and water. It was like drinking a fish smoothie!

The next day, Michelle put a small live fish in the pool. Honey Girl ignored it.

She has to be hungry, thought Michelle. *Is she in pain? Does it hurt to eat?* Or maybe Honey Girl was just uncomfortable catching food with people around.

Unlike other seal species, monk seals spend most of their lives alone. The only time female monk seals gather in groups is when they are giving birth or nursing their pups. Since her rescue, Michelle had made sure that Honey Girl was never left alone. Maybe that's what she needed now.

Thanksgiving had arrived. The aquarium staff members were eager to be home celebrating with their families. Michelle thought this would be a good day to test her idea and give Honey Girl some time alone. She put fresh fish in Honey Girl's pool and hoped for the best.

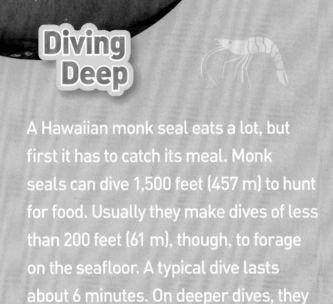

Diving Deep

A Hawaiian monk seal eats a lot, but first it has to catch its meal. Monk seals can dive 1,500 feet (457 m) to hunt for food. Usually they make dives of less than 200 feet (61 m), though, to forage on the seafloor. A typical dive lasts about 6 minutes. On deeper dives, they can hold their breath for as long as 20 minutes.

Monk seals aren't
picky eaters. They
eat a variety of foods,
depending on what they find.
Squid, octopuses, eels, and many types
of fish are all on the menu. They also eat
crustaceans (sounds like kruh-STEY-
shuns), like crabs, shrimp, and lobsters.
A monk seal can eat up to 10 percent of
its body weight in food each day.

Michelle spent the day at home with family. But she could not stop thinking about Honey Girl. Monk seals are not picky eaters. But would her injuries prevent her from eating even small fish?

Michelle couldn't wait to find out. She returned to the aquarium later that day to check on Honey Girl. When she arrived, all the fish were gone! Honey Girl had had a fine feast. "It was the best Thanksgiving I ever had and probably ever will," Michelle said.

From that moment on, Honey Girl made steady progress. She ate herring, squid, and other fish. She was starting to gain weight.

During her recovery, Honey Girl was very uncomfortable around humans. That was a good thing. In the wild, seals avoid humans. But the longer she stayed at the aquarium, the more she might get used to people. Michelle feared that she would have trouble adjusting after she was returned to the wild. "We did not want that to happen," said Michelle.

Michelle decided to ask NOAA for special permission to release Honey Girl. It was a little early. She didn't weigh as much as Michelle thought she should. But as far as Michelle could tell, Honey Girl was healthy. Michelle worried that if they didn't release her soon, she might never return to the wild. NOAA agreed, and the decision was made to go ahead.

Honey Girl nuzzles her baby on a beach.

Just under two weeks since her rescue, Honey Girl was released into the wild from Kaihalulu (sounds like ky-hah-LOO-loo) Beach. She had often been seen along this sandy stretch of beach. It had good places for her to hide, so it was a safe place for her. So safe, in fact, that she had given birth to several of her pups here.

Before the team released her, they attached a small satellite transmitter to the fur on her back. Now they could track her movements in the wild and make sure she was okay. The transmitter showed them exactly where she was swimming and how often she dived to hunt for food.

From the beach, Tracy and Michelle watched Honey Girl inch her way down to the water and into the waves. They had seen Honey Girl at her worst— injured and weak. Now she was healthier and strong.

But Tracy still worried. What if Honey Girl had another infection? What if she had trouble hunting? To be safe, she asked the volunteers to watch for Honey Girl and report back when they'd seen her.

Two weeks later, a volunteer spotted Honey Girl on a nearby beach. She looked very thin. She did not move when the volunteer came closer. *Monk seals are sound sleepers*, thought Tracy. *Is Honey Girl just asleep, or does she need help?*

Tracy, Michelle, and the NOAA team raced out to check on her. Honey Girl did not move as they approached. But, suddenly, she surprised everyone. She lifted her head, and everyone could see that Honey Girl had buried herself in the sand! She wasn't thin or injured or in trouble at all. She was snuggled deep in the sand, taking a long nap. "The sand fooled us," said Michelle.

It seemed that Honey Girl was on the road to recovery. For the first few months, the transmitter on her back showed that she was diving and hunting for food over miles of coastline, just like any other healthy seal.

One day the transmitter suddenly stopped sending signals. "It just fell off on its own, as they often do," said Tracy. But the team could still track Honey Girl by sight. And they knew that her recovery was going well.

Volunteers continued to keep an eye on Honey Girl. Within the year, they reported that she had gained back her weight and quite a bit more. *Is Honey Girl pregnant?* Tracy wondered. That would be exciting news. With so few monk seals left in the world, every birth is important.

Honey Girl had given birth to seven

pups before her injuries. Michelle hoped an eighth pup was on its way. But there was no way for them to know for sure. They would have to wait and see.

A few weeks later, another volunteer spotted Honey Girl on a beach near where she had been released. Her belly was huge, and she was moving very slowly. Two days later, Honey Girl gave birth to her eighth pup! One of the volunteers happened to be there to witness the birth. What a relief to see Honey Girl becoming a mother again! It meant she had recovered well enough to have a pup. It was a joyous day for everyone.

The NOAA team gave the pup the

Did You Know?

A monk seal's pregnancy lasts for about 330 days. Then the mother gives birth to a single pup.

number RF20. She was given the Hawaiian name Meli, which means "honeybee." Like most monk seal pups, Meli's soft fur was jet black.

Pups typically weigh about 30 pounds (14 kg) at birth. Meli's loose, velvety skin cloaked her body like an oversize coat. She needed to eat—a lot.

Honey Girl faithfully nursed Meli for six weeks. During that time, Honey Girl never left her side. Nor did she eat.

After the six weeks, Honey Girl was thinner, but Meli had a thick layer of blubber. Now Meli was old enough to be left on her own, and it was safe for

Did You Know?

A newborn pup gains more than 100 pounds (45 kg) while nursing on its mother's milk, which is rich in fat.

Honey Girl to return to the sea.

Honey Girl dived deep into the ocean. It took her only a few minutes to find and gobble up some fish. In a matter of weeks, she would gain back weight and strength.

Honey Girl's story is a story of success. The hard work of Tracy, Michelle, the NOAA team, and all the volunteers had paid off. Honey Girl had survived a life-threatening injury and had been returned to the wild in record time. Within a year, she had added another healthy pup to the endangered monk seal population. She is truly a miracle mom in a world where every monk seal birth is important. And in the end, Honey Girl finally returned to the ocean, where she was meant to be.

Saving Monk Seals

Today, Hawaiian monk seals are one of the most endangered marine mammals in the world. Although many protection efforts are in place, their population is declining. Over the past 50 years, the monk seal population has fallen more than 60 percent. Approximately 1,100 Hawaiian monk seals remain in the wild.

Hawaiian monk seals face a number of threats, like getting tangled in fishing lines, not finding enough food, and disease. Places like the Marine Mammal Center are trying to help. The Center opened the Hawaiian Monk Seal Hospital in 2014. This hospital works to rescue and care for this critically endangered species. So far, the Center has helped hundreds of monk seals.

KUZYA AND BORYA:
TIGER
RESCUE!

One of the brothers looks out of his enclosure at the Inspection Tiger Rehabilitation Center in Alekseevka, Russia.

Young Amur tigers, like this one, usually stay with their mother until they are about two years old.

Brothers in TROUBLE

November 2012
The Russian Far East

On a gray, wintry day, two orange-and-black tiger cubs wandered out of the forest. They waded through the snow, leaving a trail of footprints behind them. These were Amur (Siberian) tigers. They stayed close to the tree line, but they should not have even left the forest.

People from a nearby village would later spot the tracks and wonder, *Why would tiger cubs come so close to town?* Amur tigers live in the mountains and river valleys in this faraway part of the world. It's the only place they still roam freely. But the tigers stay hidden to protect themselves.

The villagers told the wildlife inspector who patrolled the area about the tiger tracks. He worked for Inspection Tiger, the Russian agency in charge of protecting Amur tigers and their forest home. The inspector studied the paw prints. Given their size, these young tigers were perhaps four or five months old. *Tigers that young should be with their mother. It is likely that poachers have killed her,* the inspector thought. It's against the law in Russia to kill and sell rare wild cats. Yet he knew that poachers could be paid a lot of money for a tiger's body parts or skin. These are used in Asian medicines or for decoration. Female tigers with young cubs become easy targets for poachers. The cubs cannot run fast, so their mother stands her ground to protect them.

The inspector worried about the cubs being on their own. He knew they needed their mother to survive. He also knew it was dangerous for the cubs to be seen by humans. These cubs needed rescuing.

The inspector called Dale Miquelle (sounds like mi-KELL). Dale is an Amur tiger expert. He directs the Wildlife Conservation Society's (WCS) Russian Program. For many years, Dale and his staff have rescued Amur tigers who are injured or in trouble. Tracking the biggest cats in the world is dangerous work. Tigers fascinate Dale, but he never loses sight of the fact that "they can eat us."

The search team set off on foot to find the cubs. The inspector soon spotted them and took a video with his cell phone. The video would help people know what the cubs looked like. That way, people could tell him if they spotted the cubs. That was good, because before the team could catch up with them, the cubs disappeared into the forest again.

The team knew that the cubs must be hungry. They were too young to have learned from their mother how to hunt for food. She would have hidden them in a safe place and brought food back to them.

Colossal Cats

Tigers are the biggest cats in the world. Amur tigers are the biggest type of tiger. An adult male stands about 3 feet (1 m) tall at the shoulder. This isn't quite as tall as a lion, but Amur tigers are longer and usually weigh more. A male can grow up to 11 feet (3.4 m) from nose to tail and weigh more than 600 pounds (272 kg). Females are usually a little smaller.

The team needed to reach the cubs soon, but tracking them down took much longer than anyone thought it would. For ten days, Dale and his team followed the cubs' tracks. They trudged through forests and fields of deep, crusty snow. At night, when the temperature dropped below freezing, the team would stop searching. At first light, the search would begin again.

Finding the cubs became even harder when the cubs did something that surprised the team. They split up. "You would usually capture cubs together, or at least close to each other," said Dale. Yet these two had gone their separate ways.

This meant that the search team had to split up, too. Finally, the team got a lucky break. One cub had wandered onto a military base. A bus driver spotted him. The team was able to give the cub some medicine to make him sleepy so they could capture him. They named him Kuzya, after the man who found him. Kuzya was taken to the Inspection Tiger Rehabilitation Center in Alekseevka (sounds like alex-EVE-kah).

One cub was safe, but the other cub was still missing. It took two more days for Dale's team to capture the cub they named Borya. He was hiding under a mound of brush in a snow-covered field. His orange, white, and black coat blended in with the snow, dry leaves, and tree branches. He was practically invisible to the team.

The team lured Borya out of his hiding place. They used a forked stick they had found along the way. One of the team members distracted Borya with the stick. Dale quickly gave medicine to the frightened cub to make him sleepy.

The team needed to act fast. They only had about an hour before the medicine wore off, and there was much to do. They carried Borya to a truck and drove to a house in the village to examine him. The cub looked thin. His ribs were showing. His temperature was dangerously low. The team put hot water bottles around him to raise his temperature. They injected fluids under his skin to rehydrate him.

The next morning, Dale and the staff moved Borya to be with his brother. Now Borya and Kuzya were together again. The Inspection Tiger Rehabilitation Center had been built for orphaned tiger cubs. It was a place to prepare them to be returned to the wild. It would be the brothers' home for a year and a half.

During their time at the Center, the tigers would need to learn how to hunt. This would take some practice. "It's a little bit like figuring out a puzzle," said Dale. "They instinctively know what they need to do, but they need to practice to put all the pieces together."

And if the two tigers were ever to be released into the wild, they would also need to keep a healthy fear of humans.

Two young Amur tigers sit together in the snow. They are used to living in a cold climate.

Chapter 2

Practice Makes PURRFECT

For the first few weeks, Kuzya and Borya lived in a cage in a small cabin at the Center. Here, they could eat and rest. Kuzya and Borya got to eat deer or boar meat every day. This was the same kind of food that their mother would have hunted for and shared with them in the wild. Tiger cubs need a lot of food. A hungry cub can eat 6 pounds (3 kg) of meat a day. When they arrived, Kuzya weighed 55 pounds (25 kg). That's roughly the size of a female Labrador retriever. Borya weighed a little more.

At the Center, the staff brought food and water to the cabin. As soon as the cubs heard someone approach, they hid. Tigers learn at a young age to stay away from humans. Orphaned tigers are even more cautious (sounds like CAW-shus) because they don't have their mothers to protect them. The staff used a sliding door to deliver food so the cubs did not see them.

Only one person was allowed to get close to Kuzya and Borya. That was wildlife veterinarian (sounds like vet-er-ih-NAIR-ee-en) Mikhail Alshinetski

(sounds like MEEK-hail al-shih-NET-ski).
Mikhail is the Moscow Zoo's chief
veterinarian. His job was to make sure the
cubs were healthy and gaining weight.

Giving a tiger a checkup isn't easy.
First, he gave the cubs medicine to put
them to sleep. Then he took their
temperature and measured their length and
weight. He checked their skin, fur, and
teeth. He took blood samples. He also gave
them vaccinations against diseases.

Within a month, the cubs began to put
on weight. They were moved outside to a
small enclosure (sounds like in-KLOH-
zhur) and then to a much larger area that
was surrounded by a high metal fence.
There were video cameras mounted on
poles in the corners of this enclosure.

A tall tower also gave the staff a way to watch the cubs from a distance.

Now the cubs had their own territory to explore. They could climb the hill, play in the woods, or hide in a cave. The cubs were thriving. It was time for them to start practicing how to find food.

At first, the staff left small, dead prey like rodents and rabbits in different places around the enclosure. Borya usually found the prey first. He would take the first bite and then share the rest with his brother. "Borya was the more confident tiger. At the beginning, he did everything first," said Mikhail. But it was clear that Borya and Kuzya looked out for each other.

There were three other orphaned tigers at the Center. Each had its own enclosure.

At seven months old, Kuzya and Borya still shared an area. In the wild, sibling cubs stay together with their mother until they are two years old. As long as they were getting along, the staff thought it was healthier for them to be together.

By summer, Kuzya and Borya had turned a year old. They were beginning to behave like adult tigers. They were active from morning to night. They bathed in a ditch. They hid in the tall grass. They chased each other's tails. They marked their territory by urinating along the fence. In the evening, they each picked a spot to watch the other orphaned tigers and each other from a distance.

Cold-Climate Cats

Amur tigers have to be tough to survive the harsh winter environment where they live. Extremely cold temperatures and deep snow are common. Luckily, their bodies are adapted to cold. Amur tigers have a special layer of fat on their sides and bellies that helps keep them warm. Their coats help, too. Their fur is long and thick. Like most tigers, Amur tigers have a thick, white ruff of fur around their necks. Amur tigers also have built-in "snow boots." This is extra fur on their paws that protects them from the cold and makes it easier to walk through the snow.

The two brothers no longer looked like cubs, either. Their bodies had changed a lot. They each weighed more than 150 pounds (68 kg). They each ate 10 pounds (4.5 kg) of food a day. Their baby teeth had been replaced with 30 adult teeth that were as sharp as knives. But were these big cats now fast enough and skilled enough to hunt live prey?

In the wild, a mother tiger takes her cubs to hunt alongside her. They learn what to do. These cubs didn't have a mother to show them. So, the staff had to help them without being seen. Instead of leaving dead prey in the enclosure, the staff now put in live rabbits and other small prey. Kuzya and Borya had to teach themselves to stalk slowly, run fast, and pounce quickly.

Next, the staff added wild boar and deer into the enclosure. The tigers were good at hunting small animals. Could they catch big prey? These are the animals the tigers would most often eat in the wild.

By December, each tiger brother weighed more than 250 pounds (113 kg). They were experienced hunters now. One kill every ten days was enough to keep them healthy and strong. They still shared food, but now Borya calmly waited his turn while Kuzya fed first.

In the spring of 2014, the tigers were 19 months old. They were old enough to be released into the wild, but were they ready? Their final test was to see what they would do when a staff member walked by their enclosure. Would the tigers make themselves invisible? Their survival in the wild depended on it.

On the day of the test, the nervous staff huddled at the top of the tower. They would watch what happened through binoculars. One of their teammates walked slowly past the enclosure. At the sound of footsteps, Kuzya and Borya froze. Their ears swiveled in the direction of the sound. They crouched down.

As the man stepped forward, the tigers moved silently and hid together. Their coats were a perfect camouflage (sounds like KAM-uh-flazh) against the dry grass and patches of snow. The man never saw the tigers. But the tigers kept their eyes on him the entire time. Kuzya and Borya had passed the test!

Kuzya peers out from the metal crate with wide eyes moments before being released back into the wild.

Chapter 3

HOME FREE

In May 2014, Kuzya and Borya were released back into the wild. Before release, each tiger was fitted with a special collar. The collar would send signals that Dale and other scientists could track.

Another orphaned tiger, a female, was also released at this time. Her name was Ilona (sounds like eye-LO-nuh). Like the two brothers, Ilona was just under two years old.

This is the age that tiger cubs typically leave their mothers to search for their own territories.

The Center had never released this many tigers at the same time. The staff was curious to see what the tigers would do once they were on their own. The first few months in the wild is the most important time in a young tiger's life. Would Kuzya and Borya stay together? Would Ilona find her own territory or share with one of the brothers? Usually, each tiger establishes its own territory. What happened next surprised everyone.

Kuzya and Borya split up immediately. As soon as his cage door was opened, Kuzya bounded off into the forest alone.

But Ilona and Borya stayed together for the first few days. The pairing did not last long, though. By the end of the first week, Borya had moved on alone.

Before, Kuzya had always been the more cautious one. Now, he covered a lot of ground. In two months' time, Kuzya traveled a distance of 125 miles (200 km). Dale wondered if he was having trouble finding prey. Then the team found the remains of a very large boar. They stopped worrying. He must be eating well.

Early in his travels, Kuzya passed through an area where another orphaned female tiger was living. Her name was Svetlaya (sounds like svet-LIE-ah). The staff wondered if Kuzya would stay.

A month later, the staff grew worried about Borya. His collar had been sending a signal from the same place for several days. Was something wrong? Was he injured or ill? The team rushed to the spot of his last signal. When they arrived, they did not see Borya. They found only wild boar remains. Borya's behavior was a little mysterious, but it appeared that he was alive and well.

Meanwhile, Kuzya continued to roam. At last, he reached the Amur River. This river separates Russia from China. For Kuzya, it marked the end of the tigers' forest habitat on the Russian side.

On the other side of the river lay a mix of oak trees and Korean pines. Pinecone nuts and acorns are what red deer and wild boar eat. These animals are an Amur tiger's favorite foods. Now Dale understood. "That is where Kuzya was heading," said Dale. He was looking for more prey.

The river is not easy to cross. But Kuzya leaped into its fast-moving waters. Using his great strength, he swam across to China. Over the next few months, he wandered through the forests there.

Kuzya left behind evidence that he was eating well along the way. Dale and his team thought that Kuzya had finally found his own territory. But this tiger surprised them again.

In the fall, Kuzya circled back to the Amur River. He was looking to cross back into Russia. At that time of year, the river was filled with sharp pieces of floating ice.

It was too dangerous for Kuzya to try to swim across the river now. There was too much ice. So, he headed back to the mountains to wait.

By winter, the Amur River had frozen completely. Kuzya was determined to cross. Plodding over the thick and slippery ice, he carefully crossed the river back into Russia.

Once there, Kuzya wandered into the tigress Svetlaya's territory again. Dale and the team wondered what that meant. By three years of age, Amur tigers are fully grown. They are able to mate and have cubs of their own. Perhaps Kuzya and Svetlaya will share this territory for a while, the team

Did You Know?

Tigers are good swimmers and can swim nearly four miles (6 km) in one stretch.

thought. Perhaps these tigers will start a family together.

Today, Borya and Ilona have each found their own separate territories in Russia. All four tigers continue to thrive.

Yet Amur tigers are endangered. There are only about 450 left in the wild.

Borya, Kuzya, Ilona, and Svetlaya are great success stories. Each was rescued and successfully released back into the wild. That means it's possible to return tigers to places where they had once disappeared.

"Tigers resonate with everyone in the world," said Dale. "When we learn the alphabet, we learn that *T* is for 'tiger.' It's part of our being. If we can save tigers, we may have a chance to save ourselves." So far, Dale and his team are off to a good start.

Cause an Uproar

Tigers aren't the only big cats in trouble. Lions, cheetahs, leopards, and other big cats are threatened, too. Their territory is being taken up by humans, and their food sources are disappearing. Sometimes these hungry cats try to eat people's farm animals. That puts them in danger. People try to protect their livestock and end up hurting or killing big cats. People want the big cats to stay away, but the cats have no place to go.

But there are also people who are trying to help save these big cats. That's why National Geographic launched the "Big Cats Initiative" (sounds like in-NI-she-e-tev). It's a program to raise awareness of some of the challenges big cats face. It also hopes to help humans and big cats live together.

Learn how you can help big cats, too. To get involved, start here: animals.nationalgeographic.com/ animals/big-cats-initiative/get-involved/

KASS AND DRAEGON: RHINO RESCUE!

A helicopter flies low over several rhinoceroses to see if they might be good candidates for the airlift.

A mother rhinoceros and her calf walk along the grassland in search of a watering hole.

Chapter 1

Thinking BIG

February 2015
South Africa

The day was hot and muggy on the African savanna. A female white rhinoceros nibbled hungrily on some tufts of grass. Beside her, her young calf shook off a pesky fly. The fly was circling above the two small horns on the calf's nose. Mother and son rhino ambled along in the tall grass.

They had wallowed in mud earlier at the watering hole to cool their skin. Now mud-caked, they paused for a moment in the baking sun. All was quiet.

Suddenly, the sound of a helicopter cut through the hazy sky. The mother rhino lifted her head. A rhino has poor vision, but can hear sounds that are very far away. She could not tell where this noise was coming from, though.

The calf stood still and watched as his mother looked anxiously around. The sound grew closer and louder. Was this sound a threat? A rhino's natural instinct is to avoid danger.

But there was nowhere to hide. The rhinos began to run.

There was no way for the rhinos to know that they were not in danger. There was no way for them to know that they were actually being rescued. A veterinarian (sounds like vet-er-ih-NAIR-ee-en) and a pilot were aboard the helicopter. They're part of a group called Rhinos Without Borders.

This group has a bold plan to protect rhinos from poachers and help prevent rhino extinction (sounds like ek-STINK-shun). Rhinos are in serious trouble. There are fewer than 22,000 of them in the world. More than 1,000 African rhinos are shot and killed by poachers each year.

black rhino

Rhinos

There are five rhino species on Earth.
Two of the species that live in Africa are
the black rhino and the white rhino. Both
of these rhinoceros species are actually
gray. They are different not in color, but
in the shape of their lips. The black rhino
has a pointed upper lip. The white rhino
has a squared lip. This difference is related
to what the animals eat. Black rhinos are

white rhino

browsers. They get most of their food
from trees and bushes. They use their
upper lips to grab leaves, twigs, and fruit.
White rhinos graze on grasses. They walk
with their enormous heads and squared
lips lowered to the ground. The white
rhino's name came from mispronouncing
the Dutch word *wyd* (sounds like WIDE)
to describe its upper lip.

Poachers cut off rhino horns and sell them for thousands of dollars. The people who buy the horns grind them up for "medicine" or make them into dagger handles. At the rate rhinos are being killed, there will be no free-roaming rhinos in Africa within five years.

That's where National Geographic Explorers Dereck and Beverly Joubert (sounds like jhoo-BEAR) come in.

The Jouberts are award-winning filmmakers who have been filming, researching, and exploring in Africa for more than 30 years. Their mission is to save the wild places of Africa and to protect the creatures that depend on them.

Over time, the Jouberts have learned how important all animals are to the land. In 2009, the Jouberts founded the "Big Cats Initiative" with National Geographic.

This program aims to stop the rapid decline of wild cats—like lions, leopards, tigers, jaguars, and cheetahs—around the world. The program has seen a lot of success. Now the Jouberts wanted to use what they learned with Big Cats to help save the African rhino.

South Africa has more rhinos than any other country in Africa. South Africa also has more poachers. The Jouberts came up with a daring plan: What if they could move 100 rhinos away from South Africa to a place where poachers could not find them? Then the rhinos would be safe.

The Jouberts decided that the best place to relocate them would be Botswana.

Dereck and Beverly live in Botswana. They know this country well. They also know about the people who live there. "Botswana wants rhinos," said Dereck. "And it has the lowest poaching rate in all of Africa." The laws against poaching are very strict there. Botswana would be a safer place for the rhinos.

It took a year of talking and planning for the two countries' governments to agree to the Jouberts' plan. The Jouberts also had to talk to the people whose job it is to protect endangered animals when they are being moved from one country to another. They teamed up with andBeyond and Great Plains Conservation, two safari companies in Botswana. These companies care about animals. They could use their knowledge and care to help make the project a reality.

The plan would be expensive. It would cost several million dollars. People from all over the world started giving money to help. By February 2015, the Jouberts and the Rhinos Without Borders team had raised enough money to move the first ten rhinos. How were they going to choose which rhinos would be the first to make the journey? And, more importantly, how do you get a rhino to move?

Did You Know?

The word "rhinoceros" comes from the Greek *rhino* (nose) and *ceros* (horn). Some rhino species have two horns while others have one. White rhino horns can grow up to five feet (1.5 m) long.

A pregnant female rhino is gently blindfolded to minimize stress. The team handles each rhino with care as they prepare the rhino for transport.

Chapter 2

FLYING on Their FEET

A rhinoceros can't fly. But the first ten rhinos in Dereck and Beverly's plan were going to have to. The best way to safely move the rhinos was to transport them by air. But first, the Jouberts needed to decide what sort of rhinos they were looking for.

The rhinos needed to be in good health to survive the move. The trip was going to be stressful for them.

If they were healthy and strong, the journey to their new home would not be as hard for them.

Dereck and Beverly also had to think of the future. "We want more females than males," Dereck said. This would give the rhinos the best chance of having more babies in their future home. "We don't separate mothers and calves, of course."

They also wanted to include small groups of rhinos that were moving around and grazing together. Most rhinos don't live in family groups, but they do form communities. The Jouberts didn't want to break up any of the rhino communities that were already living in South Africa.

A researcher on the team had been studying the rhinos in the area. The researcher had a pretty good idea of which rhinos might be right for the project. So, the pilot and veterinarian took to the sky on that day in February to search for the first ten rhinos. That's when the pilot spotted the mother rhino and her calf.

To his eye, this mother looked healthy. Her calf looked old enough to have been weaned from nursing. The pilot flew in closer to get a better look. The vet on board agreed. These rhinos were the right combination to take to a new home in Botswana.

The pilot didn't want to spook them. So, he backed the helicopter away. The running rhinos slowed to a trot. The pilot made one more pass. The vet leaned out the window with a dart gun. He shot a dart into each rhino's thick backside. The darts were filled with a drug that made them sleepy. Eight minutes later, both rhinos fell asleep.

A crew on the ground quickly moved in with trucks. These trucks carried large metal crates in the back to help move the rhinos. As soon as the team reached the rhinos, they placed earplugs in the rhinos' ears. Then they blindfolded each rhino with a wet cloth. The blindfold and the earplugs kept the rhinos calm. The blindfold also kept the rhinos' eyes from drying out.

The vet did a quick medical checkup on each rhino. Blood samples were taken. A treatment was given to the rhinos to prevent ticks and parasites.

What Do Rhinos See?

Unfortunately, rhinos don't see very much. Rhinos are known for their keen senses of hearing and smelling, but their vision isn't so good. Rhinos are thought to be extremely nearsighted. That means they can see better up close than far away. Rhinos can't see in color the way humans and some other animals can. In addition, a rhino's eyes are on the side of its head, so it has a hard time seeing straight ahead. A rhino's poor vision sometimes causes it to panic at strange smells and sounds. Watch out when that happens: A rhino will charge!

Once these tasks were completed, the vet gave the rhinos another drug to wake them up just enough that they could stand. With a firm tug on a rope and a team of people pushing from behind, the mother rhino and her calf walked themselves into the metal crates.

Ten rhinos were captured from different areas of the park that day. They were driven to a protected area where they would stay for six weeks. During this quarantine (sounds like KWAR-en-teen) period, they would be fed well and examined by veterinarians from both South Africa and Botswana.

Did You Know?

Rhinos, elephants, and hippos are some of the largest animals in the world. But they are all megaherbivores. That means they eat only grasses and plants, not meat.

No one wanted the South African rhinos to make the Botswanan rhinos sick. "The last thing we want is to have one of our rhinos coming in and infecting an entire population in Botswana," said Dereck.

The rhino mother and calf were given the names Kass and Draegon (sounds like DRAY-gun) by a generous donor to Rhinos Without Borders. The donor had helped to pay for their move. Kass and Draegon were placed together in a large boma, an enclosure (sounds like in-KLOH-zhur) surrounded by a tall fence. The rhinos were fed a special mix of food to help them build their strength. The rhinos were not hand-fed. "We try to limit the human interaction as much as possible," said Dereck.

But the team did encourage interaction

between the rhinos. Kass and Draegon soon discovered that another mother-and-son pair were in the same boma with them. The two pairs bonded immediately.

At the end of the six-week quarantine period, all ten rhinos passed a final health check. The rhinos had gained weight. The Jouberts were not surprised by this. "In the wild, animals are eating and moving constantly," said Beverly. In captivity, they did not have to roam very far to find their next meal. It was time to get the rhinos moved and settled in their new home.

Earlier, four microchips, each the size of a pinhead, had been implanted in the rhinos' horns and ankles. Before the next step of their journey, a radio transmitting device was fitted to each rhino so that they could be tracked after their release.

Once the rhinos were ready to be
moved, the vet gave each
rhino a tranquilizer
(sounds like TRAIN-
kwe-lize-er) to make it
drowsy. The rhinos
needed to be alert enough
to stand during the two-
hour flight but still be
calm.

The ten drowsy rhinos were walked into
their crates and were loaded onto trucks.
The trucks took them to the airport. There,
the crates were carefully loaded into the
hold of a gigantic military plane. Finally, the
rhinos were on their way to their new home.
Next stop, Botswana!

The team helps load a blindfolded rhino into a crate.

Chapter 3

Running FREE

Two hours later, the huge airplane carrying the ten rhinos and the crew landed safely at the Maun (sounds like MOW-UUn) airport.

A two-hour drive in any direction from Maun leads to a wilderness of forest, river, or desert where wild animals freely roam. Which of these wilderness areas would the new rhinos call home?

It was late morning when the crew loaded the still sleepy rhinos in their crates onto trucks. The plan was to release them into the wild right away. This is called a "hot release."

The team had mapped out the territories in Botswana where they knew that rhinos were already living. They wanted to release the South African rhinos on the fringes of those territories. "As long as there is an existing marking or boundary, they can establish their territory beyond that," said Dereck.

Once the crates were settled on the flatbed trucks, the Jouberts took off in a helicopter. From the air, they could film and photograph the last leg of this momentous journey as well as scout ahead for potential poachers.

On the road below them, the convoy of ten trucks was escorted by armed guards. Together, they began a hot, dusty, six-hour journey deep into the Okavango Delta.

The two-lane highway soon became a one-lane road. The convoy passed through fields of golden grasses. Here, the trees stuck up from the flat land like lollipops.

Suddenly, one of the trucks lurched sideways. A wheel came spinning off the axle of the truck that was carrying Draegon. The driver leaped out of the truck to make sure he wasn't hurt. Draegon seemed fine, but the truck wasn't. Luckily, there was room in the back of the truck carrying Kass to fit Draegon's crate. It took an hour to lift the one-ton (0.9-mT) youngster onto the truck with a crane.

At last, the convoy was ready to move again. By then, it was afternoon. The heat was sweltering, and the air was humid. And there was more trouble ahead.

It was the end of the rainy season, and flooding was common in the Okavango Delta. The convoy had to cross several rivers that were much higher than normal. Each time they crossed a river, crew members took turns guiding the trucks through the high water. In some places, the water reached five feet (1.5 m) deep.

It was close to sundown when the driver in the first truck saw a shimmering line of water stretching along the horizon. Was it another river to cross, or had they finally reached their destination?

Did You Know?

Three of the five rhinoceros species are listed as being critically endangered.

As the crew drove closer, they saw islands of tall grasses. They saw the dark figure of an elephant walking along against an orange sky. They saw herds of antelope and impala drinking at the water's edge. A vast wilderness lay before them. It had everything the rhinos would need to thrive.

The convoy came to a stop. By sunset, the crates were off-loaded, and the first of the rhinos stepped out. Most of the rhinos walked calmly out of their crates and into the wilderness. But not all.

One of the males came charging out in a cloud of dust. The crew stood still so they would not attract attention. He soon settled down once he realized there was no danger. Kass and Draegon joined the other mother and calf and began grazing peacefully together.

Someday, when Draegon gets older, he will leave Kass and head out to find his own territory. Male rhinos need larger territories than females do. But if Kass has a daughter in the future, she will keep her mother company until she is grown.

For now, this is the safest place for the rhinos to be. It's a wide wilderness with few roads for poachers to use to find them.

And they will be watched over. A security team from Botswana will carefully keep an eye on all of the rhinos. The rhinos will also be watched over by a well-trained anti-poaching team.

Against all odds, the Jouberts and the Rhinos Without Borders team moved the first ten African rhinos to safety. They fought against the dangers of poachers and the huge cost of their operation, and they worked within the politics of two governments. "It was important to take action on a species that was being targeted," said Beverly.

Over time, the rest of the 100 rhinos will be airlifted and released at different locations in Botswana. Where the first ten rhinos were released remains a secret to this day. The Rhinos Without Borders crew members want it to stay a secret, too. This first big step toward helping rhinos was successful. Kass and Draegon, along with eight other healthy rhinos, are finally running free.

Rhinos Without Borders

Rhinos Without Borders wants to help stop rhino poaching in Africa. It has committed to moving 100 rhinos from high-risk areas in South Africa to safer locations in Botswana. The project has another goal, too. It aims to increase the geographical spread of the rhino population throughout southern Africa and introduce new rhino genes into Botswana. There is still much work ahead for the Jouberts, their crew, and the African rhinos.

THE END

DON'T MISS!

NATIONAL GEOGRAPHIC KiDS **CHAPTERS**

HOOT, HOOT, HOORAY!

And More True Stories of Amazing Animal Rescues

Ashlee Brown Blewett

Turn the page
for a sneak preview . . .

Baby owl Paul stands beside his sister, Babe. Eastern screech-owls can be red, like Paul, or gray, like Babe.

PAUL AND BABE: HOOT, HOOT, HOORAY!

When Homer Kuhn found these little baby owls, their eyes were still closed.

Chapter 1

May 1, 2013
New Creek, West Virginia, U.S.A.

It was a sunny day, without a cloud in the sky. Birds chirped, squirrels barked, hawks screamed, and a family of deer ate grass near the edge of the woods. Woodcutter Homer Kuhn (sounds like COON) had just finished sawing the base of a dried-out tree.

"Timber!" Homer called.

The tree hit the ground. *Thud!*

Homer looped a long, heavy chain around the log. His brother, Willie, pulled the log out of the forest using a large machine that looks like a tractor, called a skidder. As the log slid past Homer, a flash of white caught his eye. He thought he saw two snowballs lying on the ground. But Homer knew that they couldn't be snowballs. It was 80°F (26.5°C) outside.

Homer says, "I thought, what in the world is lying white like that in the middle of the woods?" He walked over to investigate. Lying in the dirt were two baby eastern screech-owls.

Homer scooped up the baby owls, or owlets, in his hand. They looked like two fluffy marshmallows. *Peep, peep!* the owlets called. *They must have fallen out of a hole in the log,* Homer thought.

Some birds build nests. Not screech-owls. Instead, they nest inside tree cavities (sounds like KAV-uh-tees). These are holes made by other animals, like woodpeckers. Usually, the mother owl looks after the babies while the father owl hunts for food to bring back to the family.

Homer searched the area for the owlets' parents. He looked inside the holes of other trees. But he found no parent owls. Homer knew that if he left the owlets in the woods with no home and no parents, they would die. He wrapped the babies in an old T-shirt. Then he pulled his cell phone out of his pocket and called the one person he knew would help.

"Hello," said Mrs. Tammi Kuhn.

"Hi, Mom," Homer answered. "We have something."

"Is it squirrels again?" Mrs. Kuhn asked.

"No, we found two baby owls this time," Homer said.

"Oh my!" said Mrs. Kuhn. "I'll be right there."

Mrs. Kuhn was used to getting calls like this from her sons. Homer and Willie work for a logging company. They spend most days in the woods, cutting down trees. Then they sell the logs they collect to a nearby sawmill to be cut into boards and sold as lumber. Sometimes, in the woods, the brothers find baby animals.

Owls, Owls, Everywhere

Owls live on every continent except Antarctica. They come in many shapes and sizes. The Eurasian (sounds like yur-AY-zhun) eagle-owl can grow to more than two feet (0.6 m) tall. It can weigh up to ten pounds (4.5 kg). The elf owl only grows to around six inches (15 cm) tall. It weighs less than half as much as this book. Owls' feathers help them blend into their habitats. The snowy owl's thick white feathers hide it from enemies in the frozen Arctic. And the gray- and rust-colored feathers of a screech-owl make it seem to disappear next to a tree.

Eurasian eagle-owl

"If we find baby squirrels or baby raccoons, we try to rescue them," Homer says. "We find a lot of squirrels." When the boys spot these animals, they call their mother for help. "She raises them until they are old enough to care for themselves," says Homer. Then Mrs. Kuhn returns the animals to the wild.

Mrs. Kuhn has raised and released many squirrels over the years. But screech-owls were different. She had never cared for screech-owls. In fact, it is illegal to raise them in West Virginia. But these babies needed help.

Mrs. Kuhn got in her car and drove to the edge of the woods. "I really didn't know what to do with baby screech-owls, but I didn't want them to die," says

Mrs. Kuhn. She called everyone she knew, trying to find a rescue center that could take

them. Meanwhile, she drove the owlets back to her house. She put them in a box with a heating pad to keep them warm, and she did her best to feed them.

In the wild, baby screech-owls stay in the nest for about one month. Then they begin to learn how to fly and hunt. After that, the parents continue to protect and feed their young owls for two or three more months, until they can hunt on their own. But the baby owls' eyes were still closed. They were less than a week old.

Want to know what happens next? Be sure to check out *Hoot, Hoot, Hooray!* Available wherever books and ebooks are sold.

INDEX

Boldface indicates illustrations.

MORE INFORMATION

To find more information about the animal species featured in this book, check out these books and websites:

National Geographic Animal Encyclopedia
by Lucy Spelman, 2012

Tigers in the Snow
by Peter Mathiessen, 2001

International Fund for
Animal Welfare
ifaw.org (Amur Tiger)

Hawaiian Monk Seal
Research Program
www.pifsc.noaa.gov/
hawaiian_monk_seal/

Hawaiian Monk Seal
Volunteer Network
monksealmania.blogspot
.com

Rhinos Without Borders
greatplainsfoundation.com

Save the Rhino
savetherhino.org/rhino_info

Wildlife Conservation Society
wcsrussia.org
(Amur Tiger)

CREDITS

**To Dan for his
endless patience and support, and
to Donna for her careful wordsmithing. —C.H.M.**

ACKNOWLEDGMENTS

Thank you to the following people who so graciously shared their time and expertise with me. The book would not have been possible without you.

Beverly and Dereck Joubert, National Geographic explorers-in-residence and founders of Rhinos Without Borders; and their trusty assistant Verity Sullivan

Dale Miquelle, director of the Wildlife Conservation Society's Russian program and fearless Amur tiger expert

Gail A'brunzo, International Fund for Animal Welfare's Animal Rescue manager, for taking and running with my cold call; Mila Danilova, IFAW's Russian office for tracking down and translating information about the tiger brothers' rehab; and Mikhail Alshinetski, chief veterinarian at the Moscow Zoo

NOAA Marine Mammal veterinarian Michelle Barbieri; NOAA scientist Tracy Mercer; NOAA Response Team volunteer Lesley MacPherson; and Honolulu Zoo's veterinary surgeon for helping to find and to save Honey Girl

Rachel Sprague, Dr. Charles Littnan, and Jeff Walters at NOAA's National Marine Fisheries Service for educating me about Hawaiian monk seals

I would also like to thank my agent Anne Depue and my editors, Shelby Alinsky and Brenna Maloney, along with the entire National Geographic Kids Books staff, who helped make this book possible.